Searchlight
BOOKS™

What Can
We Do about
Pollution?

How Can We Reduce

Transportation

Pollution?

L. J. Amstutz

Lerner Publications ◆ Minneapolis

Content Consultant: Steven Cliff, Research Professor, Air Quality Research Center, University of California, Davis

Lerner Publications Company
A division of Lerner Publishing Group, Inc.
241 First Avenue North
Minneapolis, MN 55401 USA

For reading levels and more information, look up this title at www.lernerbooks.com.

Library of Congress Cataloging-in-Publication Data

Amstutz, Lisa J., author.
  How can we reduce transportation pollution? / by L. J. Amstutz.
     pages cm. — (Searchlight books. What can we do about pollution?)
  Includes bibliographical references and index.
  ISBN 978-1-4677-9515-9 (lb : alk. paper) — ISBN 978-1-4677-9707-8 (pb : alk. paper) — ISBN 978-1-4677-9708-5 (eb pdf)
1. Transportation—Environmental aspects—Juvenile literature. 2. Automobiles—Environmental aspects—Juvenile literature. 3. Air—Pollution—Juvenile literature. 4. Automobiles—Motors—Exhaust gas—Environmental aspects—Juvenile literature. I. Title.
  HE147.65.A47 2016
  363.73'1—dc23
                        2015032756

Manufactured in the United States of America
1 – VP – 12/31/15

Contents

Chapter 1

TRANSPORTATION POLLUTION

Cars, trucks, planes, trains, and ships carry people and goods all over the world. More than one billion cars are on the road. And that number is growing fast.

Cars are a major source of transportation pollution. How many cars are on the road?

Motorized vehicles make our lives better in many ways. But they come with a cost. Transportation pollution is all the harmful waste these vehicles create.

SIMILAR TO OTHER VEHICLES, PLANES PUT HARMFUL GASES INTO THE ATMOSPHERE.

A car's exhaust is only one type of pollution the vehicle creates.

Types of Transportation Pollution

There are three main types of transportation pollution. Making and disposing of vehicles causes pollution. Also, vehicles' engines give off emissions that pollute the air. Vehicle noise is another type of pollution.

All of this pollution can harm plants, animals, and humans. The good news is scientists are working hard to solve the pollution problem. And as you will see, you can help too!

Choosing transportation that creates less pollution is one way to help solve the problem.

Chapter 2

MANUFACTURING AND DISPOSAL

Many materials are needed to make vehicles. They include glass, rubber, steel, and plastic. But where do these things come from? They begin as raw materials in the earth.

A car's body is usually made of steel. What are some other materials needed to make a car?

Some raw materials are removed from the earth by mining or drilling. These processes can release small particles into the air. Also, chemicals used in mining can leak into the water supply. Mining and drilling can damage land as well.

Large machines dig for iron. This metal is used to make steel.

Factories turn raw materials into usable forms. Other factories shape these materials into vehicles. These processes create more pollution. For example, making a new car from raw materials can produce up to 39 tons (35 metric tons) of carbon dioxide. That is nearly one-half of the pollution the car will create in its lifetime. And it all happens before the car drives a single mile!

STEEL PRODUCTION PUTS LARGE AMOUNTS OF CARBON DIOXIDE INTO THE ATMOSPHERE.

Sometimes parts that could be reused are left to rot in landfills.

When a car reaches the end of its life, more pollution is created. Seven percent of a car's lifetime pollution comes from its disposal. About 80 percent of a car is recyclable. But other parts must be thrown away. So, at least 20 percent of a car ends up in landfills.

Mines can leak pollution into bodies of water. A copper mine in Romania caused damage to this lake.

Effects of Manufacturing and Disposal Pollution

When particles from mining get into the air, people and animals breathe them in. This can cause diseases of the lungs and throat. Chemicals in the water supply can poison drinking water. This makes people sick. Land damaged by mining may become unlivable for wildlife or plants.

Carbon dioxide is a greenhouse gas. Greenhouse gases trap the sun's heat in our atmosphere and warm the earth. They make our planet warm enough for life. But too much of these gases causes problems. Because of them, Earth's average temperature has risen 1.4 degrees Fahrenheit (0.8 degrees Celsius) in the past one hundred years. And it continues to rise.

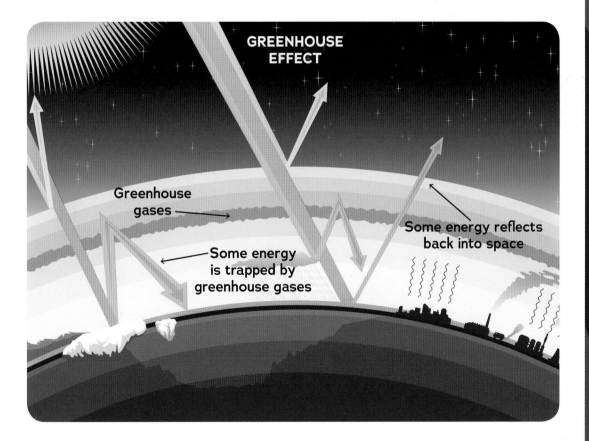

GREENHOUSE EFFECT

Greenhouse gases

Some energy is trapped by greenhouse gases

Some energy reflects back into space

Earth's rising temperature leads to climate change. Polar ice caps are melting, and sea levels are rising. Strong storms and heat waves are becoming more common. Some areas are becoming drier, making it harder for plants and animals to live there.

Car parts in landfills can also pollute the soil. This pollution can get into lakes and rivers as well.

CLIMATE CHANGE HAS A WIDE VARIETY OF EFFECTS, INCLUDING DROUGHT.

Solutions for Manufacturing and Disposal Pollution

When a car finally stops running, people should recycle as much of it as possible. Metals, glass, rubber, and some plastics can be melted down and reused. That means fewer raw materials have to be mined or drilled. Making more parts recyclable would also reduce the amount of waste. Building new cars from recycled material reduces pollution as well. For example, using recycled steel cuts water and air pollution by one-half.

To help reduce manufacturing pollution, people should take good care of their cars and use them for as long as possible. This way, fewer new cars will have to be built.

Chapter 3

AIR POLLUTION

Vehicles are a major source of air pollution. In cities, there are many vehicles in a small area. They can make the air dangerous to breathe.

Big cities have millions of vehicles. What can these vehicles do to the air?

There are several kinds of air pollution. Smog is one kind. It forms when gases from vehicle exhaust mix with sunlight. This smelly haze hovers over many large cities. It is worst on calm, sunny days when there is no wind to blow it away.

Los Angeles, California, is one city that suffers from smog. Much of this smog is caused by the large number of cars in the city.

Large trucks often release clouds of diesel soot.

Particulates are another kind of air pollution. When engines burn gasoline or diesel fuel, they do not use it all up. Tiny pieces of fuel and gases are left over. These particulates escape into the air through the exhaust pipe. These can be solid or liquid. Solid forms include dust, ash, soot, and other materials. Some contain the poisonous metal lead. Liquid fuel also evaporates from the fuel tank and hoses.

Not all air pollution stays near the ground. Carbon dioxide goes into the atmosphere when cars burn fuel. Other gases mix with water droplets in the clouds. This mixture falls to the ground as acid rain.

Acid rain can cause major damage to trees.

What Effects Does Air Pollution Have?

Your body needs lots of clean air to stay healthy. Plants and animals need clean air to breathe too. That is why air pollution is so dangerous. In 2012, air pollution caused seven million deaths worldwide.

IN CITIES WITH BAD AIR POLLUTION, SOME PEOPLE WEAR MASKS.

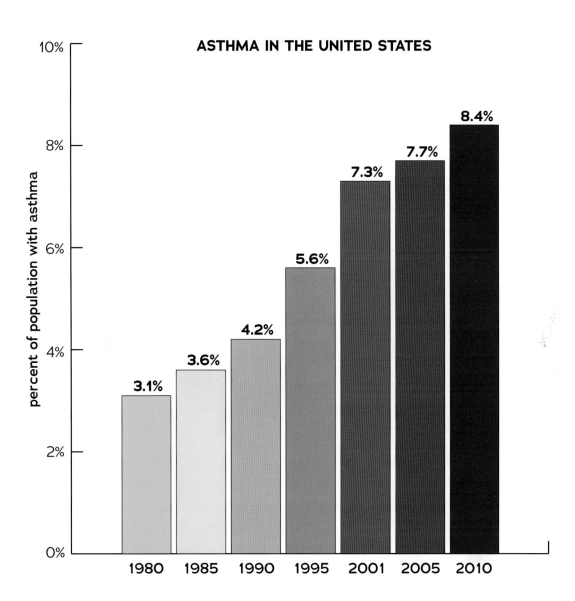

ASTHMA IN THE UNITED STATES

percent of population with asthma

- 3.1% — 1980
- 3.6% — 1985
- 4.2% — 1990
- 5.6% — 1995
- 7.3% — 2001
- 7.7% — 2005
- 8.4% — 2010

Smog causes asthma and other breathing problems. It can irritate eyes and skin. It can also damage organs and even cause cancer.

Like smog, particulates can make people sick. The smaller the particle, the more harmful it is. Tiny bits work their way deep into the lungs. They make it hard to breathe. They can also affect the heart.

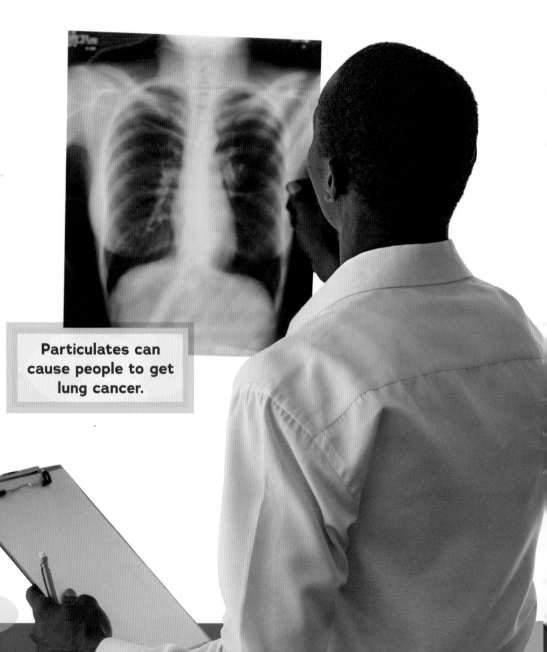

Particulates can cause people to get lung cancer.

A scientist studies a rock in a dead lake. In a healthy lake, this rock would have organisms living on it.

Pollutants in the atmosphere have harmful effects as well. Carbon dioxide contributes to climate change. Acid rain damages leaves, bark, and soil. It can kill entire forests. In ponds and lakes, acid stops fish and frog eggs from hatching. It eats away at the shells of shrimp and other animals. When predators eat these animals, they get sick. Soon the lake becomes a dead zone. There are thousands of dead lakes around the world.

How Can We Fight Air Pollution?

The Clean Air Act of 1970 has reduced emissions in the United States. Today's cars are 90 percent cleaner than those built in 1970. New truck engines are cleaner as well. Smog is less of a problem in many US cities.

New car parts can reduce the amount of particulates that vehicles emit. These parts can be fitted to a vehicle after it is made. They can reduce particulates by up to 95 percent.

A CATALYTIC CONVERTER IS A CAR PART THAT KEEPS MANY HARMFUL GASES FROM ENTERING THE ATMOSPHERE.

Hydrogen fuel-cell cars do not emit any carbon dioxide.

The best way to reduce carbon dioxide emissions is to drive less. New fuel sources can help too. For instance, fuel-cell cars run on hydrogen instead of gasoline or diesel fuel. Only water comes out of the exhaust pipe.

Trees take in carbon dioxide and give off oxygen. So, they can help take extra carbon dioxide out of the air. By planting more trees and not cutting down forests, people can help reduce carbon dioxide in the atmosphere.

Limestone is usually ground into tiny pieces before it is added to polluted lakes.

Lakes and soil damaged by acid rain can be treated with lime. Lime comes from a rock called limestone. It cancels out the acid. But this solution is temporary. The acid level in the water will eventually return. A better solution is to prevent acid rain from forming at all. The Acid Rain Program of 1990 created stricter laws in the United States. It has helped reduce harmful gases.

Transportation planning can cut down on air pollution as well. Cities can build safer sidewalks, crosswalks, and bike lanes. These make it easier for people to walk or bike. Walking and biking also make people healthier. A few cities have even banned cars from downtown areas. This approach is called smart growth. The idea is to have housing and transportation options closer to where people work and shop. That way, people do not have to travel far for everyday activities.

When cities create bike lanes, more people usually ride bikes on those streets.

Chapter 4

NOISE POLLUTION

Do you live near railroad tracks, an airport, or a busy highway? If so, you may suffer from noise pollution. Noise pollution is unwanted sound made by transportation.

People who live near airports often hear unwanted noise. What are some other sources of noise pollution?

Noise pollution does not only happen on land. It can happen in the ocean too. Ship and submarine engines make lots of noise. These vehicles also use sonar. This is a way of using sound waves to measure distances underwater.

NOISES FROM SUBMARINES CAN DISTURB ANIMALS THAT LIVE IN THE SEA.

Why Is Noise Pollution a Problem?

Noise pollution can cause stress and headaches. It can also lead to hearing loss. It can affect sleep too.

Lack of sleep can cause people to get sick more often.

Whales use sound to communicate with other members of their groups.

Underwater noises harm marine animals, including whales. These animals rely on sonar to hunt and navigate. Some animals starve or get lost. Others panic and dive deeper than their bodies can handle.

Many cities put tall, thick walls between highways and houses. This reduces noise pollution.

Preventing Noise Pollution

The best way to prevent noise pollution on land is to build fewer roads. The more highways expand into areas where people live, the more people will be affected by noise. Another solution to noise pollution is traffic planning. Cities can limit the size and speed of vehicles near homes. Trees and fences block some of the noise from busy roads.

Quieter jet engine designs cut down on noise pollution in the air. Scientists are working on new silent aircraft. The shape of these planes will make them quieter and more efficient. Also, new high-speed trains could replace short flights. This would be a quieter and cleaner option.

Government agencies are beginning to look at ways to cut down on noise pollution in the ocean too. Perhaps in the future, stricter laws will help save the lives of marine animals.

JAPAN HAS HIGH-SPEED TRAINS THAT CAN TRAVEL MORE THAN 250 MILES PER HOUR (400 KILOMETERS PER HOUR).

Chapter 5

HOW YOU CAN HELP

Vehicles put pollution into the air, water, and soil. This harms humans, plants, and animals. Scientists are working to solve the pollution problem. You can help too! Even small changes can make a big difference.

Walking is a great way to reduce transportation pollution. What are some other options?

Every mile driven puts nearly 1 pound (0.5 kg) of carbon dioxide into the air. Choose to walk or bicycle when possible. For longer trips, or in bad weather, take a bus or train.

Buses save fuel by carrying many people at once.

There are other ways you can help remove extra carbon dioxide from the air. You can plant trees around your home, school, or neighborhood. The trees will help clean the air.

Planting trees is not only good for the air. It also makes an area more beautiful.

LET YOUR REPRESENTATIVES KNOW WHY YOU CARE ABOUT TRANSPORTATION POLLUTION.

Writing letters or e-mail is another way to help. Let your political representatives know your thoughts. Tell them what you have learned about pollution. Transportation pollution is a serious problem. But if we work together, it is a problem we can solve!

Glossary

acid rain: rain that contains acids. These acids form when pollution from burning fuel combines with water droplets in the clouds.

asthma: a disease of the respiratory system. Symptoms include wheezing, coughing, and shortness of breath.

climate change: a long-term change in the earth's climate

dispose: to get rid of

emissions: gases that come out of a vehicle's exhaust pipe

evaporate: to change from a liquid into a vapor. Gasoline evaporates from fuel tanks and hoses and goes into the air.

exhaust: steam or gases given off by an engine

greenhouse gas: a gas that traps radiation from the sun near the earth's surface

particulates: very small bits of material given off when fuel burns

pollutant: any substance that harms the air, water, or soil

predator: an animal that feeds on other animals

recycle: to treat or process materials so they can be reused

smog: a mixture of smoke, fog, and pollutants. Smog forms a haze that can cause illness or even death.

sonar: the use of sound waves for finding direction

LERNER

SOURCE

Expand learning beyond the printed book. Download free, complementary educational resources for this book from our website, www.lerneresource.com.

Learn More about Transportation Pollution

Books

Feinstein, Stephen. *Solving the Air Pollution Problem: What You Can Do*. Berkeley Heights, NJ: Enslow Publishers, 2011. Feinstein explores a number of strategies for improving the quality of our air.

Flounders, Anne. *Getting from Here to There*. South Egremont, MA: Red Chair Press, 2014. This fascinating book explains the environmental benefits of various forms of transportation.

Lawrence, Ellen. *Dirty Air*. New York: Bearport Publishing, 2014. Vivid photos and hands-on activities help readers understand air pollution.

Websites

AirNow
http://www.airnow.gov/index.cfm?action=aqikids.index
Interactive games make this website a great tool for learning about air quality.

Clean Air Kids
http://www.clean-air-kids.org.uk/airquality.html
This website explains a variety of environmental effects that air pollution can have.

Smog City
http://www.smogcity.com/
Learn about the effects of smog and what you can do about it on this informative site.

Index

Photo Acknowledgments

The images in this book are used with the permission of: © huseyintuncer/iStockphoto, 4;
© travellight/Shutterstock Images, 5; © matteo69/iStockphoto, 6; © Anna Bryukhanova/
iStockphoto, 7; © RicAguiar/iStockphoto, 8; © ValterCunha/iStockphoto, 9; © Webeye/iStockphoto,
10; © Clint Spencer/iStockphoto, 11; © Florin Stana/Shutterstock Images, 12; © daulon/
Shutterstock Images, 13; © DrRave/iStockphoto, 14; © Alinute Silzeviciute/Shutterstock Images, 15;
© Luciano Mortula/Shutterstock Images, 16; © trekandshoot/iStockphoto, 17; © Andy Ryan/Getty
Images, 18; © Marek Mnich/iStockphoto, 19; © testing/Shutterstock Images, 20; Red Line Editorial,
21; © legenda/Shutterstock Images, 22; © Lara Neel/Traverse City Record-Eagle/AP Images, 23;
© typhoonski/Thinkstock, 24; © Jose Gil/Shutterstock Images, 25; © Jenoche/Shutterstock Images,
26; © Jorge Salcedo/Shutterstock Images, 27; © Steve Heap/Shutterstock Images, 28; © alxpin/
iStockphoto, 29; © Justin Horrocks/iStockphoto, 30; © MR1805/Thinkstock, 31; © carroteater/
iStockphoto, 32; © YMZK-Photo/Shutterstock Images, 33; © Imagesbybarbara/iStockphoto, 34;
© MonkeyBusinessImages/Thinkstock, 35; © Claudiad/iStockphoto, 36; © filiz76/iStockphoto, 37.

Front Cover: © iStockphoto.com/JohnnyH5.

Main body text set in Adrianna Regular 14/20.
Typeface provided by Chank.